W for Web

Restrictions on Alteration

You may not modify the Book or create any derivative work of the Book or its accompanying documentation. Derivative works include but are not limited to translations.

Restrictions on Copying

You may not copy any part of the Book unless formal written authorization is obtained from us.

Learn tomorrow skills TODAY

with TomorrowSKILLS.COM

About the T for Technology Series

Are you too young to modern technologies and feeling like sometimes you can't even follow what is discussed on the internet? Or have you already seen some in school but are still feeling frustrated because there are still so many difficult languages you have never seen? In the modern digital era there are many new words and phrases popping up on a daily basis. These new language stuff tend to be flexible and way less formal. Still, they can become fairly easy to learn if there are straight forward explanations available to get you started. This is exactly what we have prepared for you here – plain-English introduction of the fundamental tech terms you need to know to survive the 21 century classroom.

This book focuses on web related tech words and phrases.

Table of Contents

operating system

It is the most important program that runs on a computer. Every computer must have an operating system to run other programs. It performs all the basic tasks.

It is often being referred to as "OS". All software programs run on top of an OS.

multitasking

All modern operating systems are multi-tasking and multi-user capable.

On a multi-user system, one user cannot interfere with another user's activities.

All modern server OSs are capable of multitasking.

process

A process refers to a program being executed. Each process has its own descriptive information structure known as process control block. This is something rather technical....

Each application has at least one process. It can have many more.

file system

It is a structure that keeps track of the way files are organized on the disk drive. You can think of it as a hierarchical collection of files and directories that make up an organized, structured set of stored information you can retrieve if needed or wanted.

cms

Short for Content Management System, it is an application suite that allows administrators to create and manage content as well as to operate the website.

A full scale CMS is usually based on a file system on the server which connects to a database.

social media

Social media is a term that describes computer-mediated technologies for facilitating the creation and sharing of less formal information such as ideas, hobby interests and other forms of expression. Facebook is an example.

hashtag

Visually it is just a word or phrase preceded by a pound sign. In the context of social media, it is often used to identify message and draw attention on a specific topic.

web 2.0

This term describes the second generation of web services, which are way more user-friendly and interactive, with highly collaborative and participatory facilities available for users to generate more contents.

user-generated content

This term refers to posts, comments, photos, music and videos ...etc etc that are generated by users through all online interactions.

moderated

When users post comments, the comments are being reviewed and acted on prior to getting published.

client

To make things simple, just keep in mind an end user is always a client. A client always enjoys services provided by others.

A client can be a desktop computer, a notebook, a mobile phone or a pad device. Software programs for daily use run on the client side.

server

A server is a way more powerful and resourceful computer that is dedicated for providing services to you.

A regular user seldom needs to work directly on a server. Advanced web based database systems have at least one component running on the server side.

web server

A server dedicated to the running and operation of web sites.

A web server can host one or more web sites together.

database server

A server at the backend dedicated to hosting a backend database for a web site.

ad server

It refers to a special server software that stores and displays advertisements to web site visitors. It is also capable of tracking advertisement delivery.

ctr

Short for Click-Through Rate, it is the percentage of individual users viewing a web page who click on a specific advertisement that gets shown on the page. It indicates how good the advertisement has been in capturing users' interest.

impression

Sometimes being called a view, it is a term that refers to the point in which an advertisement is displayed (merely displayed) to a visitor.

page hit

Also known as page impression, it serves as a counter for your web pages. It tells the number of times a specific web page has been accessed by a user.

hit counter

Also known as visitor counter, it is a simple script that can be used to display the number of visitors for a given web page. The counter will be incremented by one each time the web page is loaded. It may be made visible or transparent to the user.

webmaster

This term refers to the guy who manages and maintains the website.

administrator

This term refers to the guy who administers, manages and maintains the web server.

html

It stands for Hyper Text Markup Language. It is the primary programming language used to write content on the Web.

The original HTML codes can be used to produce rather static web pages.

dhtml

D = Dynamic. DHTML refers to a combination of the traditional HTML codes and the various programming languages to create more dynamic web pages.

In the past, browser compatibility was a major problem with DHTML.

html5

The latest version of HTML which is way more powerful and dynamic. It is compatible with almost all new web browsers.

xml

Modern web pages may be created via different languages. Extensible Markup Language (XML) is a general-purpose markup language which is "extensible" as it allows users to define their own tags.

java

It is a programming language. It is also a computing platform. It allows complex programs to run through the web. In fact it also runs on mobile and TV devices.

netiquette

It describes the acceptable way of communicating on the Internet in a proper manner.

avatar

It is an interactive representation of a human in a virtual environment such as the web.

ftp

File transfer protocol. A mechanism for downloading and uploading files from and to web servers.

save as

When you right click on a web link and choose Save As, you are downloading something from there.

jpeg

JPEG = Joint Photographic Experts Group. This graphic format is commonly used for photos displayed on the world wide web.

png

PNG = Portable Network Graphics. This graphic format uses lossless compression for better quality than JPEG.

gif

GIF = Graphics interchange format. It is a simple graphic file format that supports 256 colors.

flash

Adobe Flash is a platform for developing vector graphics, animation, games and other web compatible multimedia contents. There is a Flash plugin for most web browsers.

Copyright 2017 **Tomorrowskills.com**.

quicktime

This is a digital video standard developed by Apple even though it is now cross-platform compatible. A free Quicktime plugin is needed in order to view QuickTime movies.

vector graphics

Unlike painted image, these are digital images made through a sequence of mathematical statements that use lines and shapes to compute graphics.

dpi

Short for Dots per Inch, dots are in fact the smallest unit of measurement for printing out digital images.

ppi

Short for Pixels per Inch, it is also a measure of image resolution. It works according to how many pixels are present within a given section of a graphical image.

web address

It refers to the web site address. You need to know it in order to access the web site.

url

Uniform Resource Locator is the addressing system used in the World Wide Web and other Internet resources. It has information on the method of access as well as the server to be accessed.

404 error

It is a common website error message. It basically tells you that a webpage cannot be found.

It may be that you have typed in the wrong address or the link is outdated.

active link

It refers to a hyperlink currently selected in your web browser. Some web browsers show the active hyperlink with a different color.

Copyright 2017 **Tomorrowskills.com**.

anchor

It refers to non-linear links among web documents, such as a word or phrase linked to another page or resource.

hypertext

This is a term that describes the system that allows web documents to be cross-linked via hyperlinks.

hypermedia

It is all about linking to multiple media.

embedded

Linking of web contents may be embedded - instead of clicking and linking to a separate page, the linked content is shown inside the current page.

inline images

They are graphics contained inside a Web document.

mosaic

The common name of a Web multimedia browser program developed long time ago.

Copyright 2017 **Tomorrowskills.com**.

netscape

The term was used to refer to a very famous web browser software which was the standard many many years ago.

IE

Internet Explorer is the web browser that comes shipped with the Microsoft Windows OS.

plugins

It refers to addon tools for web browsers that allow you to view contents of special formats.

Plugins are usually free to download and use.

torrent

A special file that is sent via the BitTorrent protocol. It can be any type of file. Along the transmission process the file is incomplete and is therefore being referred to as a torrent.

bt

Short for BitTorrent, it is a file sharing protocol designed to distribute file transfers across multiple systems so to lessening the average bandwidth consumption.

frontpage

A very popular web authoring software many many years ago.

dreamweaver

A very popular web design software for creating dynamic web contents many many years ago.

coldfusion

As a rapid web application development platform, ColdFusion was originally designed to facilitate the connection between simple web pages and a backend database. It has its own programming language called ColdFusion Markup Language CFML.

This is not an open standard but a commercial proprietary system.

SQL

Short for Structured Query Language, it is sort of a computer language commonly used in database management and programming. You can use it to manage data stored in a relational database management system.

sql server

It is a Microsoft proprietary database system.

oracle

It is a Oracle proprietary database system.

bookmark

In the context of web design, it refers to a named location on a page which is set as the target of a hyperlink.

In the context of web browsing, it is a feature of the browser for saving the address of a favorite site.

favorite

Some browsers use the term "favorite"

to refer to a bookmarked site.

search engine

It refers to the web program that can help users find information regarding certain web sites. Google, Yahoo, Bing ...etc are examples of search engines.

submission

In the context of web searching, it means submitting a site to the search engine so that the site can be searched by users.

asp

Active Server Pages ASP is a server side scripting engine that enables the creation of dynamic and interactive web pages.

asp.net

It is a comprehensive web application framework. ASP is a technology of Microsoft.

.net

It is a framework for software development framework. Microsoft offers this framework as a controlled programming environment where software can be developed. It is Microsoft proprietary. Some software require this framework in order to run. You can download it for free from Microsoft anyway.

navigation

In the context of web design, it refers to a navigation bar that provides a standard location for placement of navigation elements. Such bar provides consistency throughout the website.

title

In the context of web browsing, a page title is what get shown in the title bar of the window when the page is viewed.

template

In the context of web design, it refers to a master copy of a web document that used to create clone pages.

style sheet

Style Sheets aka Cascading Style Sheets CSS is a feature for adding different style elements such as fonts, colors, border, tables, layouts and spacing to web pages.

Simply put, it allows you to make fancy looking sites.

inline styles

This refers to a feature that allows you to easily overwrite the default style sheet of the website by specifying a different style element.

cgi scripts

Short for Common Gateway Interface, these are codes that can be used to add features to your web site such as order forms, guestbooks, and hit counters.

CGI scripts have been available long time ago. They reside on the server and is often server platform specific.

cookies

It is a mechanism in which textual messages are sent from a website and are stored on your local computer. This is useful for customizing web pages and tracking passwords that you view or use.

This may pose some security risks.

wysiwyg editor

It means what you see is what you get. Modern web designer software programs all work this way so you do not need to manaully type HTML codes.

online editor

Some use this term to refer to web design software that can access the visual editor and the source code editor side-by-side. Some use this term to describe web design program that runs directly on the internet (you do not need to install it on your local computer).

source code

It refers to the underlying HTML codes

of a web page.

Copyright 2017 **Tomorrowskills.com**.

markup

HTML is said to be a markup language. The language is specially for the processing, definition and presentation of text and other contents in terms of formatting, layout and style.

compression

It is all about reducing a file size through eliminating excess or unnecessary data. This can be very helpful for saving large size image files.

enterprise portal

Enterprise Information Portals are special web based infrastructure which allow enterprise employees, partners and customers to search and access corporate information.

You may think of it as a gateway for users to log into and retrieve corporate information, company history and other informational resources.

edi

Short for Electronic Data Interchange, EDI refers to the transfer of data between different companies using computer networks.

EDI and Internet can be two totally different things - EDI may or may not run on the internet.

Copyright 2017 **Tomorrowskills.com**.

ebusiness

Electronic Business ("e-Business") may be thought of as the business process that relies on an automated information system running over the web.

email

With email, everything takes place electronically.

Email addresses are unique.

Email has a unique post office, which is the email server. When you send your email the last part of the address after the @ is the server address. You do need several things to send and receive email. You need an Internet connection,

an email account, and also an email

software package.

webmail

Web based email is different from traditional email.

You do not need to install any email software locally. Instead you simply use your web browser to access the email account being hosted on the service provider's server.

vpn

Short for virtual private network, a VPN is a network that is constructed by using public wires to connect hosts in different geographic locations. VPN systems use encryption and other security mechanisms for security purpose.

log in

It means the "sign in" action. Normally you must have registered an account first in order to sign into a computer system, unless the system is completely unprotected.

Advanced database systems often require their users to sign in before gaining access.

login

It may refer to the credentials you use to sign in, particularly your login name. In most cases the login is your account name.

It may also indicate the sign in action. It is quite common for computer systems to display a login button for you to click and proceed to logging in.

account

Most networked computer systems require that you first register an account in order to log in and use the services provided. Account registration involves asking you to fill in a bunch of information and specify an account name for yourself. This may be done manually by the administrator or via other means.

Copyright 2017 **Tomorrowskills.com**.

log on

It means log in.

log off

It means "sign out". You usually do this when you are about to stop using the computer. See this example: I logged off so that John could use the computer.

domain registrant

This is the entity to which a domain name is registered. This person has overriding authority over that particular domain name.

domain name registrar

This is a business specializing in registering domain names. An accredited registrar can update the domain name database by the domain name registry.

domain name registry

It is a database of all domain names and their associated registrant information in the top level domains.

top-level domain name

Known as TLD, it refers to domains at the highest level in the domain hierarchy. For example, .com is a top-level domain name. So is .net.

administrative contact

This is not about server management. This is the guy who has been authorized to interact with the domain name registrar for purposes such as renewing domain names and editing contact information.

END OF BOOK

Please email your questions and comments to
admin@Tomorrowskills.com.